Look at it Differently And create a Fractured Painting

2nd Edition

By Tiffany Budd
BA (hons) SAA UKCPS Silver GSA

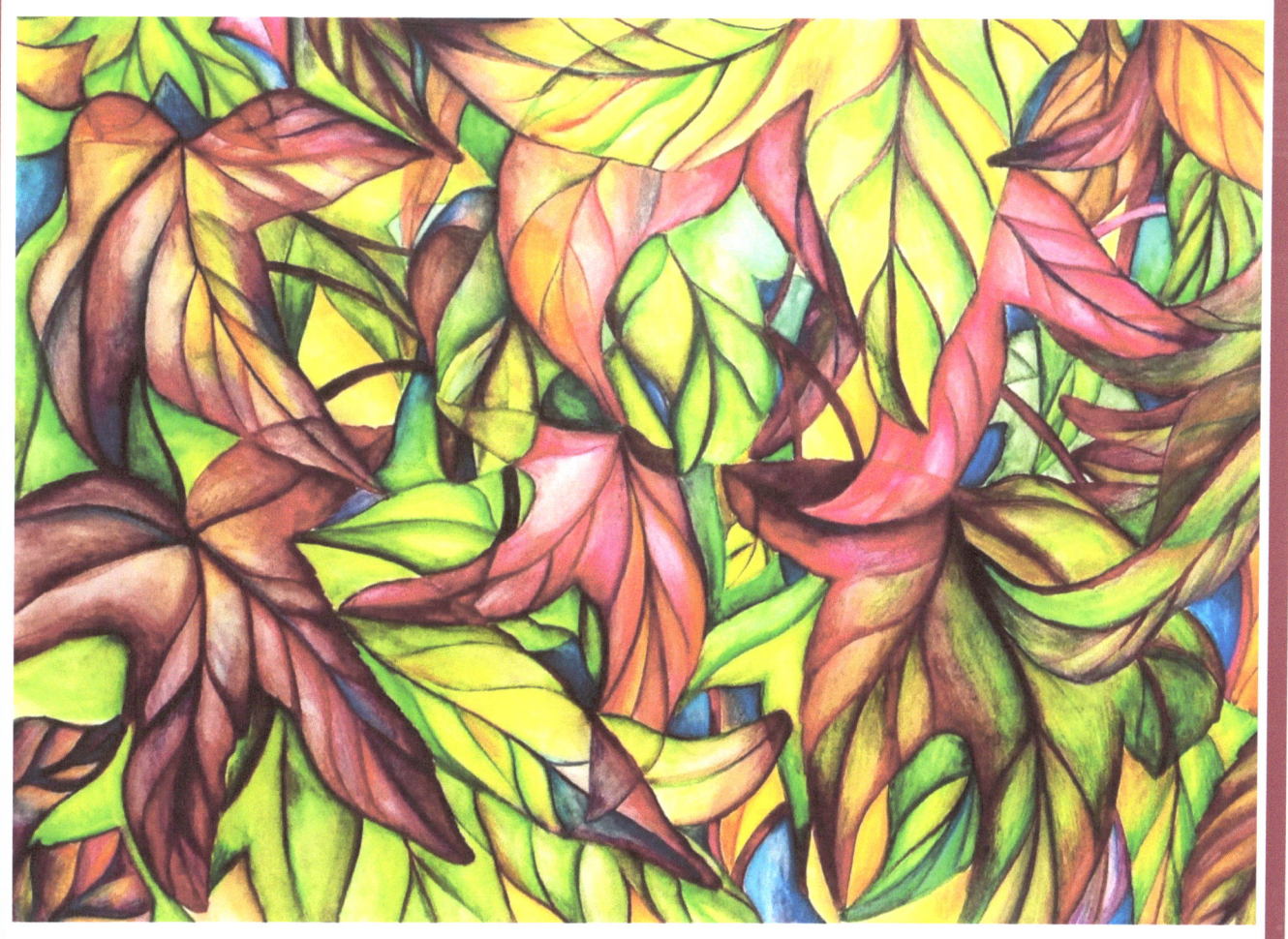

About the Author and Artist

Tiffany Budd BA (Hons) is an award winning British established fine artist, specialising in acrylic painting, coloured pencil and pastel drawing.

She studied at Wimbledon School of Art and University of Plymouth and gained a degree in Textile Design. The course included Business Studies and Fine Art. After a career in Textile Design and then Interior Design, the demand for her artwork increased so much that she became a full time artist. Tiffany's subjects vary due to the requirements of her clients, but her main subjects are florals with collage combined, Fractured paintings, and coloured pencil realism.

Tiffany has paintings published all over the world and has worked with Marks and Spencers UK on their Wall Art collection, as well as having her paintings reproduced onto ceramic tiles. She also works with an agent which licenses' her work throughout the world.

Tiffany's drawing of St Paul's Cathedral was featured on the tin lid of the new Derwent Chalk Pastel Tin, in stores worldwide. They released another collection of drawings, this time for their Coloursoft pencil product packaging and more recently, Derwent Academy coloured pencils.

She was a finalist in the New Artists Competition which was run by DeMontfort Fine Art. Tiffany exhibited at the Autumn Fair at the NEC, Birmingham.

Tiffany won The Bacchus Award painting competition, held at Denbies Wine Estate, Dorking, Surrey for her painting 'The Regret of Temptation'. Denbies has also purchased one of Tiffany's paintings, and she has had four solo exhibitions in their popular gallery.

Tiffany was awarded Highly Commended for her painting 'Harbour Boats' in the National Acrylic Painters Association exhibition, it also sold the first day.

Tiffany won a place in the Guildford Calendar, with her painting 'Stylish Guildford' in her 'Fractured' style. The painting was sold at The Surrey Artists, annual exhibition.

Tiffany came 2nd in a UK wide competition run by Caran D'Ache to create a drawing out of just 5 colours using their Museum Aquarelle pencils. It was exhibited at The Mall Galleries, London.

The 'Fractured' style of painting has been developed and recognised by the art community by Tiffany since 2002, inspired by the Cubists and Russian Constructivism, focusing on perspective and light. There has been a demand for this style of work and has sold to clients all over the world. Tiffany takes any subject and breaks it up using perspective and light direction, then enhancing the areas using different tonal values and colour. You will find out how to do it in this book!

Tiffany regularly has exhibitions of her work in the UK and worldwide, including the UK Coloured Pencil Society, St Ives, Canada, Australia, Scotland, Wales and Surrey Open Studios. Tiffany has been awarded Silver Signature status from the Society
Tiffany undertakes private commissions and works directly with the client creating a bespoke piece of art for their room schemes. She is also a member of The Society for all Artists, The UK Coloured Pencil Society, Australian Coloured Pencil Society and The Fine Art Trade Guild.

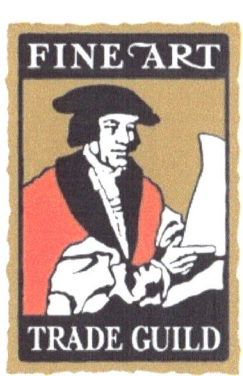

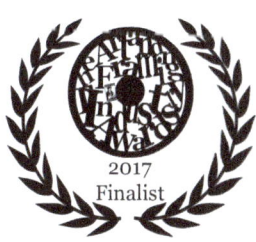

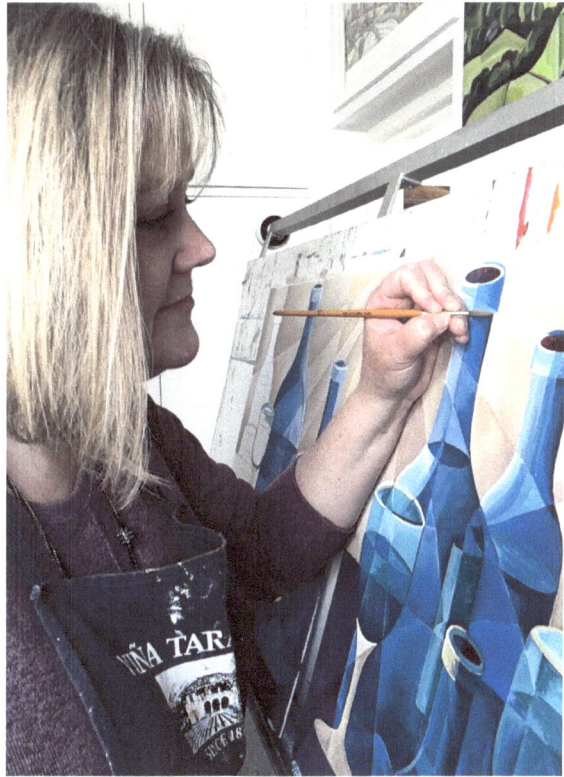

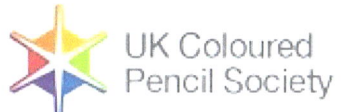

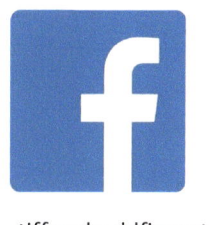

tiffanybuddfineart

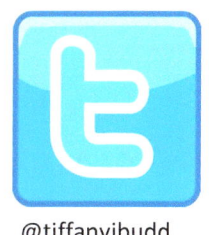

@tiffanyjbudd

My inspirations and development.

Almost all artists, at some point in their career, have the desire to create art which says, 'This is me, this is what I do'. A personal art identity if you will! That is what I was aiming for....

'Fractured', is a term I came up with after quite a few months of work.

In 2002 I saw an exhibition of the Russian Constructivists (1914-1930) at Tate Britain and was totally inspired by the strong tight lines and movement.

Cubism has also always been a inspiration for me. The combination of these two art movements led me towards my own style. The first time I created this effect, I was doodling in my sketchbook after the exhibition. I was drawing, very simply, a wine bottle and glass in charcoal. Gradually I shaded the areas to bring up the shape, shadow them interesting and beyond the usual.

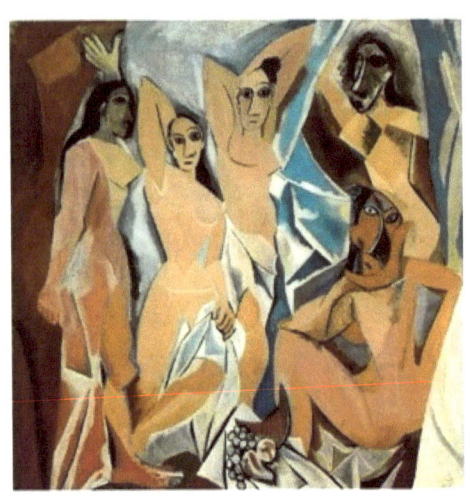

Les Demoiselles D'Avignon 1907 by Pablo Picasso- This painting began Cubism.

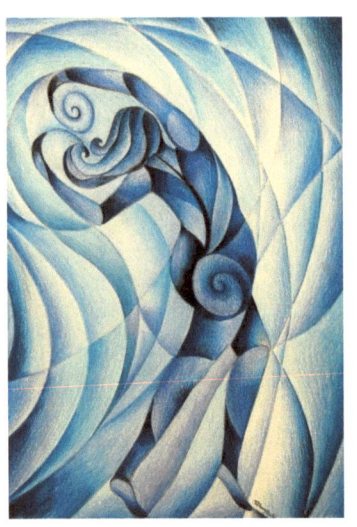

Moonlight Dancer- by Tiffany Budd My take on figurative movement using Fracturing.

Cubism is one of the first modern art movements you learn about in school and I was hooked! It was such an exciting way of working, something completely different. I think we all had to complete an art project on Cubism at some point in our Art education? I didn't stop.

It is so important to look at things differently. Of course, it has been done before. Cubism was one of the mostinfluential visual art styles of the early twentieth century. It was created by Pablo Picasso (Spanish, 1881-1973) and Georges Braque (French, 1882-1963) in Paris between 1907 and 1914.

The excitement and creativity for me, begins when you start to develop and change an image. I don't make the image unrecognisable, just make the viewer see something in a different way, so it becomes semi abstract.

I decided to call my way of working 'Fractured', so it looks like it has been broken or shattered, like glass and then put back together. I work very tightly and this sort of art suited me perfectly

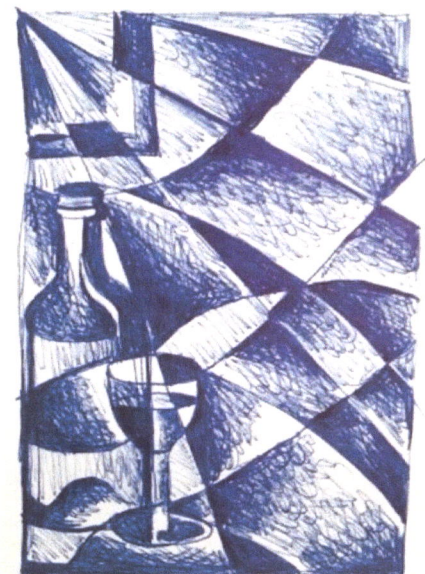

Wine bottle and glass– Biro

This is the first ever Fractured painting I did. A small sketch in biro, in my sketchbook on my way home from the Tate exhibition. I was so excited!

I focused on perspective and light but kept it a recognisable image.

It developed into 'After a Hard Day', I imagined there were streaks of light- Much like a rainbow coming through a prism- and used them in my work. I visualised light direction and how it would look if you saw it broken up using colours to create the difference in light and depth.

I like to take a traditional subject and treat it in Cubist way. Colour is very important to me when putting together these paintings.

My subjects vary- from landscapes to figurative. With figurative paintings especially, I want to create an image that looks like it's moving, trying to catch the dynamism. A visit to see the Olympic Fencing men's in 2012 was fantastic! The dynamism of their movements was an inspiration to me.

Watching the ladies Gymnastics was also brilliant. I can't bend and bounce like that let me tell you! I visualised those athletes as almost in slow motion, in a shutter action. The result of that is on the next page.

I find inspiration anywhere. My sketchbook and camera are always with me, just in case.

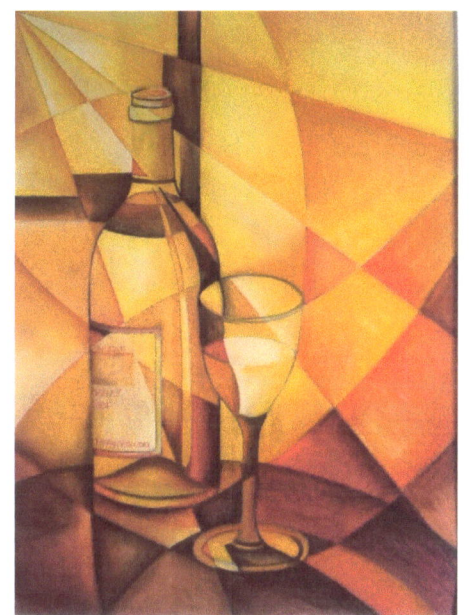

After a Hard Day– Derwent pastel

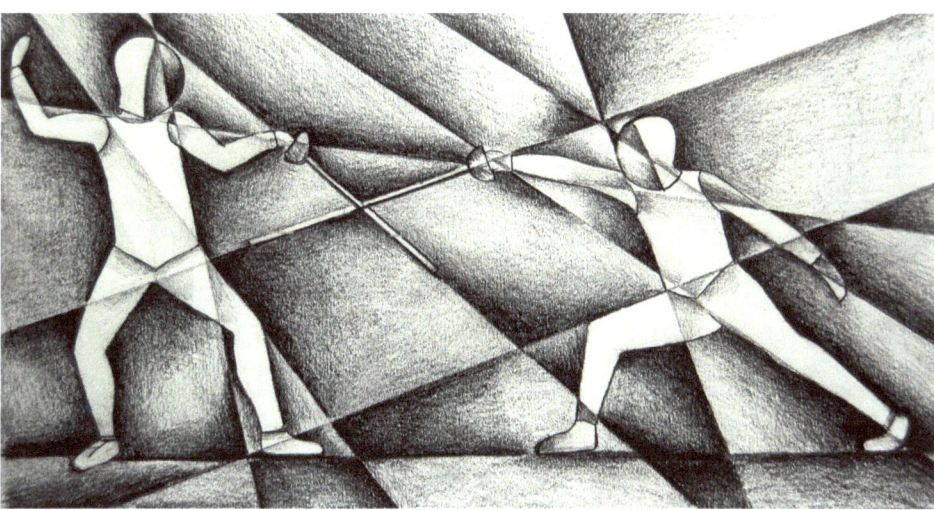

The Fencers– Graphite

With my landscapes, I like to do quirky perspectives and colour, just like the Cubists did. But I divide the landscape, either real or imaginary into sections of colour. Each section treated as an area in its own right, each as important as the next. I see beyond the obvious colour, but see the shades and light and bright colours. I believe I am a colour addict! If I see dark green in a landscape, I will use purple instead. Yellow? I'll use some orange and brown for depth. I love creating imaginary landscapes making them interesting and beyond the normal.

I imagine there are streaks of light - Much like a rainbow coming through a prism and using these lines in my artwork. I imagine light direction and how it would look if you saw it broken up. I focus on perspective and light but keep it a recognisable image.

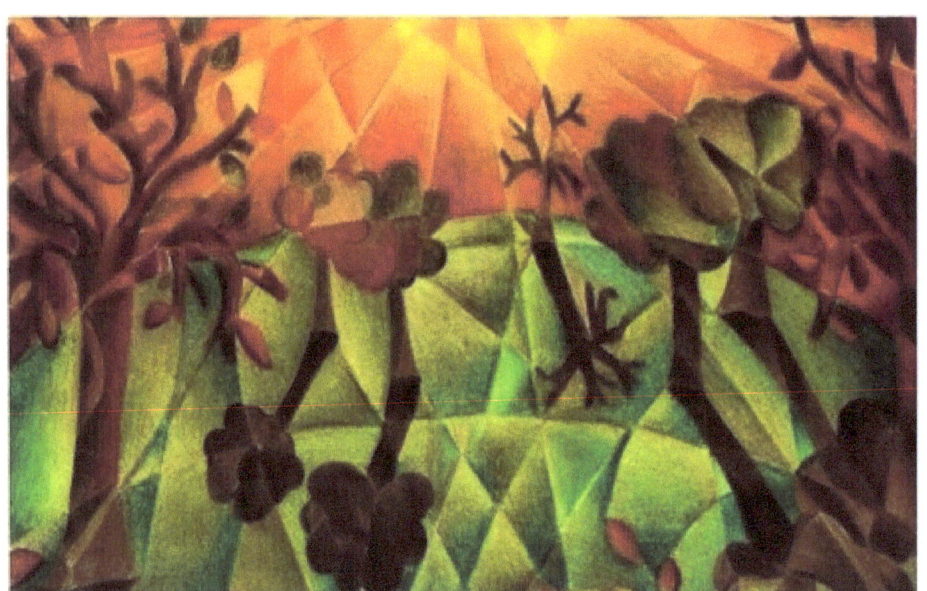

'Flaming Autumn' Coloured Pencil.

In this drawing I imagine I can see the light beams shining through the sky, casting shadows on the grass. Each beam Fracturing the landscape. I kept the colour palette traditional autumnal colours.

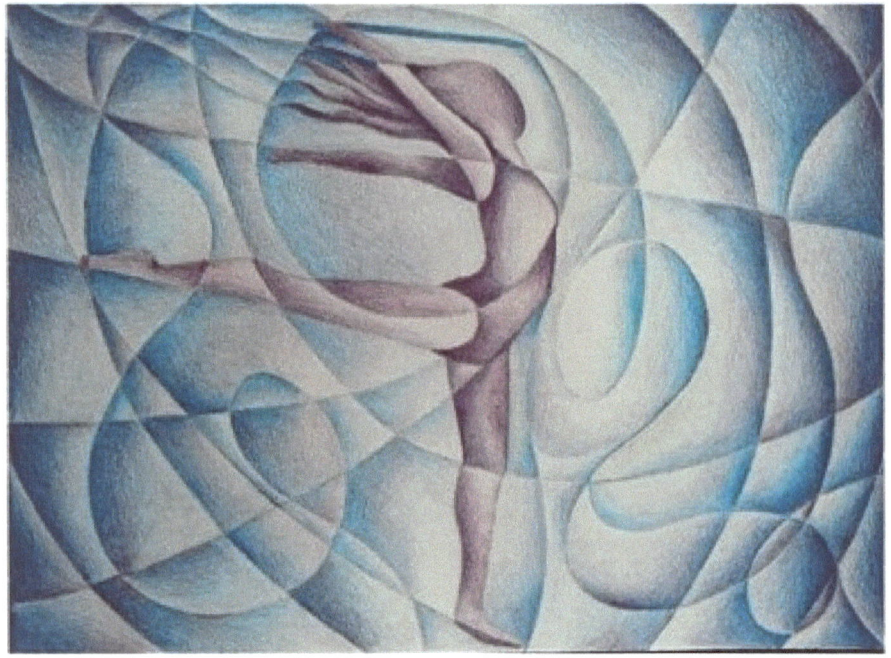

'The Ribbon Dancer' Coloured Pencil

With figures, I try and attempt to make the figure flow and move. Especially with the added movement of the ribbon. I had great fun creating this and making her dance!
The colours for this had to be calm and cool!

So, now it's your turn!
Let me guide you through a series of exercises and projects to learn how to create my type of work.

How to create the Fractured style-
Exercise 1. Getting to grips with tones.

In this chapter, I will give you an exercise using just graphite pencil, mainly to get to grips with tonal values and how each section of 'Fracture' stands out on its own, going from light to dark.

Firstly, draw an outline of a square about 8cm each side.
Divide this square up into 4 sections.
Using a soft graphite pencil (4-6B) blend from dark to light each section.
Press hard to soft from one edge to the other.

The key to making this work is, at each edge, make the depth of tone different.
Dark or light. You will see then that the square sections become more interesting and almost move. This is what Fracturing is all about!

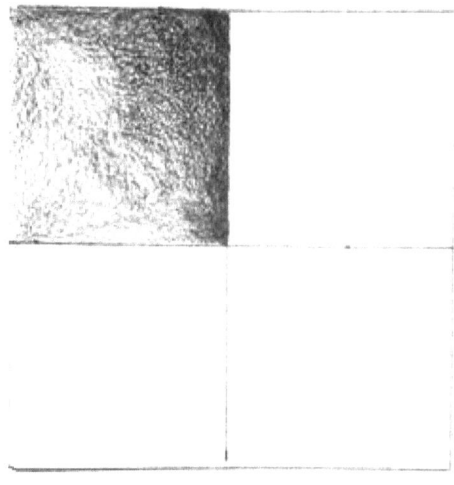

Make sure one side is darker than the other.
Get used to how the graphite blends

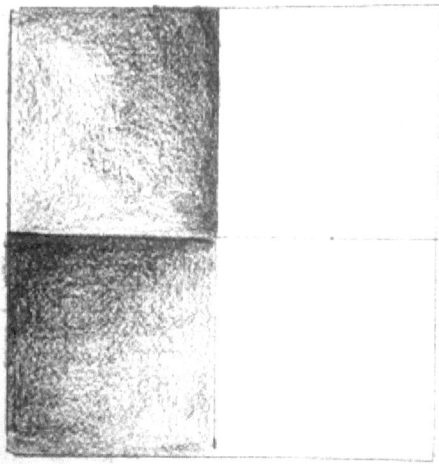

Blend the next square, keeping an eye on the next squares tones, light and shade.

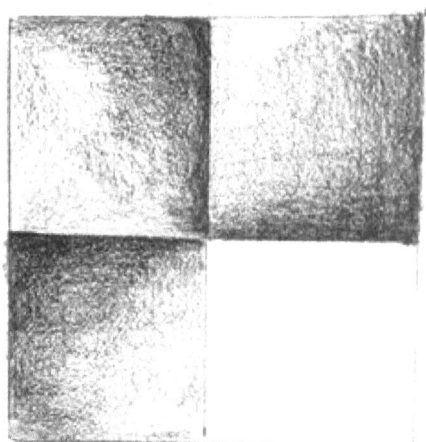

The more sections you do, the more aware you will be of how dark the edges need to be.

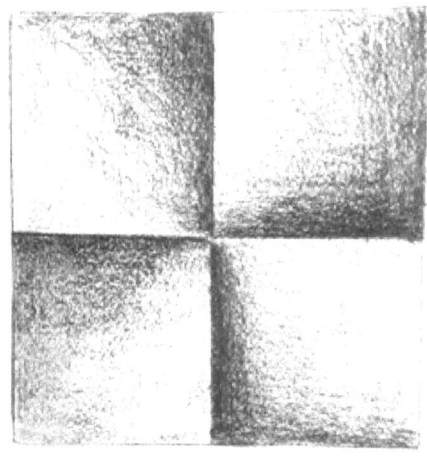

You will now see how each square works in it' own right,
At every edge there is a different tone meeting up.

Creating a simple Fractured drawing of a wine bottle and glass using graphite.

We now begin to focus on the light 'Fractures', and actual shapes.

Here we will create a black and white drawing of a still life of wine bottle and a glass.

It is best to use a soft graphite pencil like a 4B, it creates lovely soft strokes.

On the page opposite, I have drawn a simple outline of the items.

I have overlapped drawing each object and by doing this means you've started Fracturing the image already. (Fig 1)

From this we will start to add our Fracture lines, which begins to abstract the obvious shape .

Firstly, try to imagine beams of light as actual lines which fan out the further down the paper. (Fig 2)

Separate each section into a shape, not too big, not too small. I envisage a light bulb or sunlight coming from the top left of my drawing. Add shadow lines at the bottom direct from the shapes. I have added a line going upwards from the glass to break up the large section. Then add more lines off the bottle label and bottle top. (Fig 3)

Next add the tones, just like we did in the previous exercise. Start light near the top left and then gradually darken the tone. (Fig 4)

Gradually add more tones throughout the drawing. Keeping the edges sharp. (Fig 5)

Work from one section to the next to making sure each edge is contrasting.
Remember to not have the same tone along each edge.
We want each section to work in its own right, and not blend together.
Darken or lighten any areas which aren't standing out.

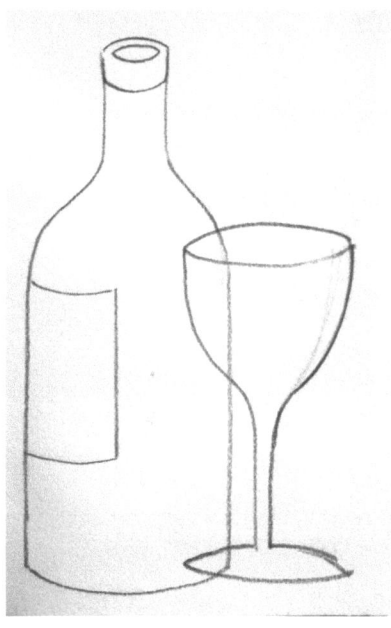
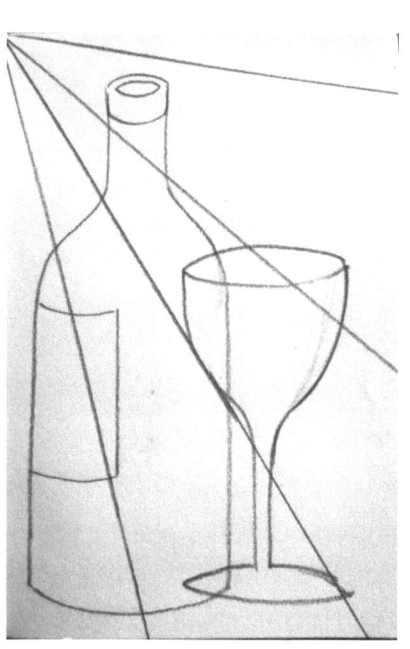

Fig1- Simply draw an outline of a wine bottle and glass overlapping the lines.

Fig 2- Choose your light direction and draw beams of light through the image.

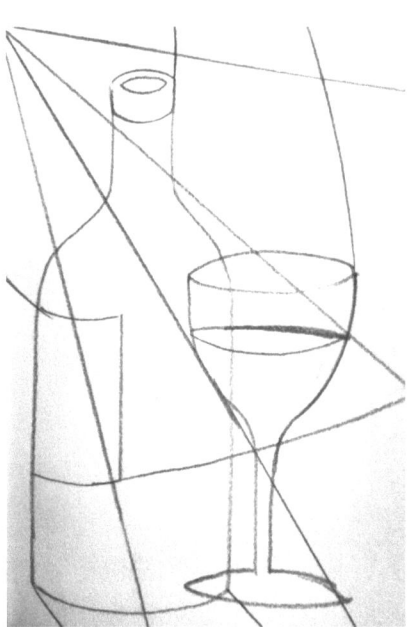
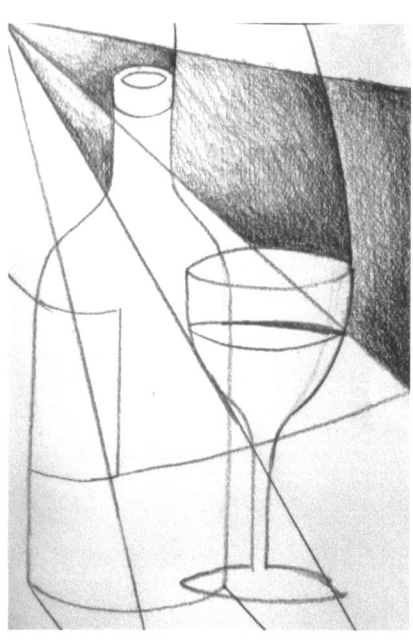

Fig 3- Begin to add on lines, coming from the bottle and glass themselves.

Fig 4- Light to dark on each section creates the Fractured look.

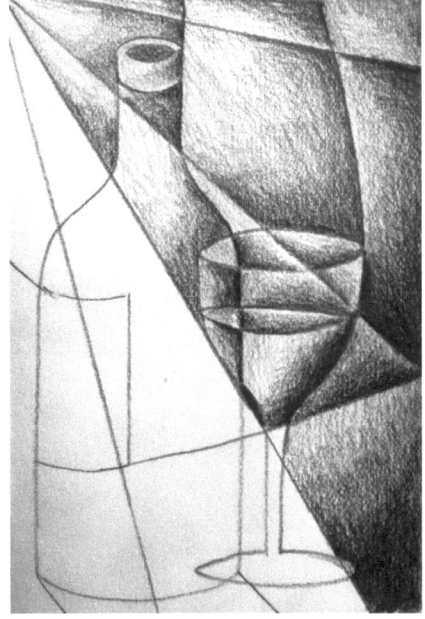
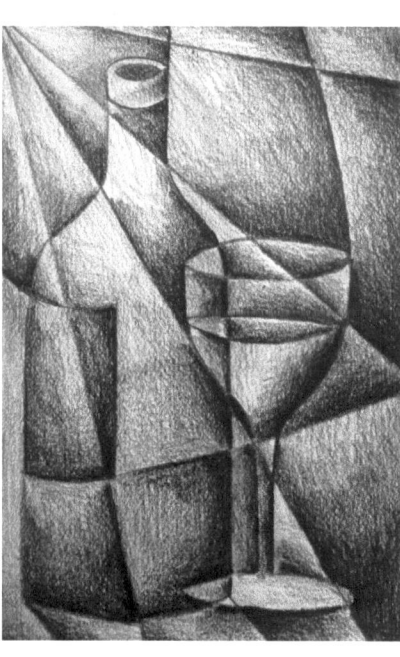

Fig 5- Make sure your pencil strokes are as smooth as possible when blending.

Deepen or lighten your tones to enhance to Fracturing for a crisp tight look.

Now lets add some colour to your drawings!

Purple bottle and glass pastel painting

For this exercise you will need:-

Pastel pencils
Pastel blocks (hard). I used Derwent Pastel Blocks.
Ruler
Smooth pale grey pastel paper (with no lines).
I completed this picture in A4 size. An ideal type of paper is a sanded one. Something like Colourfix or Pastel Mat. The tooth in the paper works extremely well with pastels and really enhances the colour.
Paper stump or sponge pastel blender.

The colours we will be using are:-
Pink, Indigo, Cerulean, grey, white, pale pink, lilac, cyan and purple.

You will notice that they are all the same tonal values of blues and cool colours. This is to achieve the look of the objects and background being as important as each other.

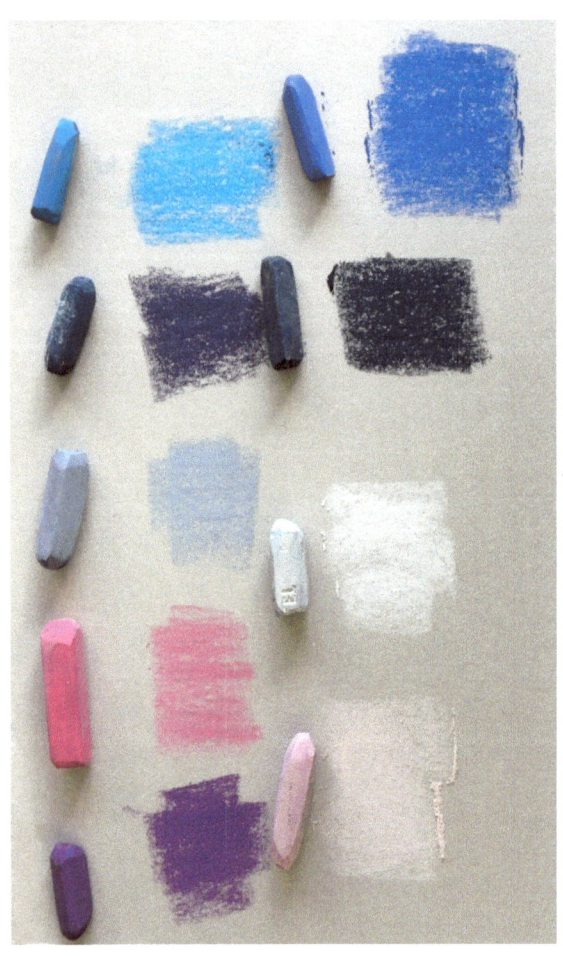
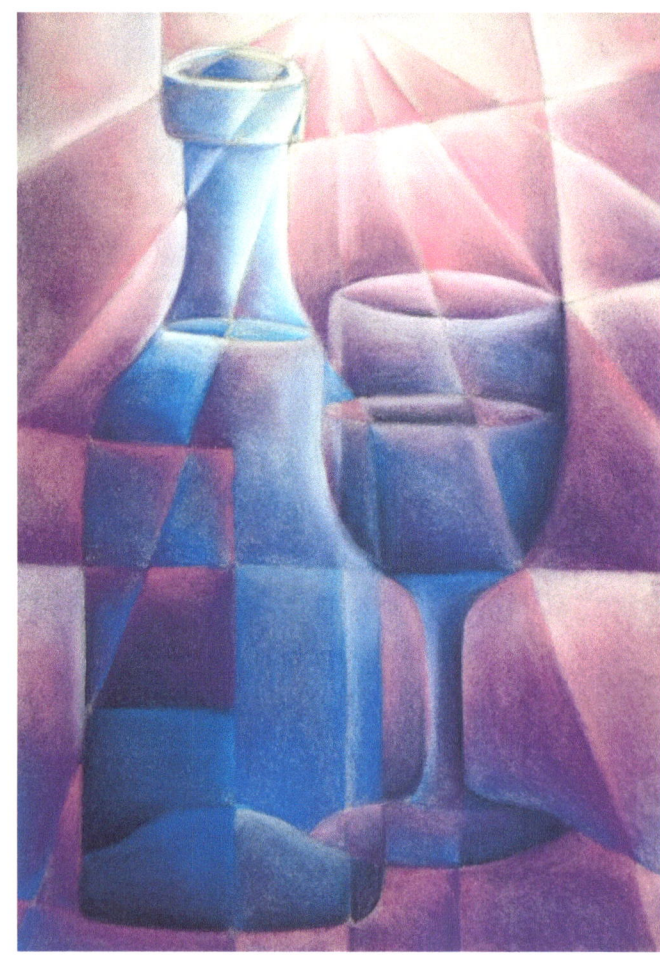

Developing the Fractures

 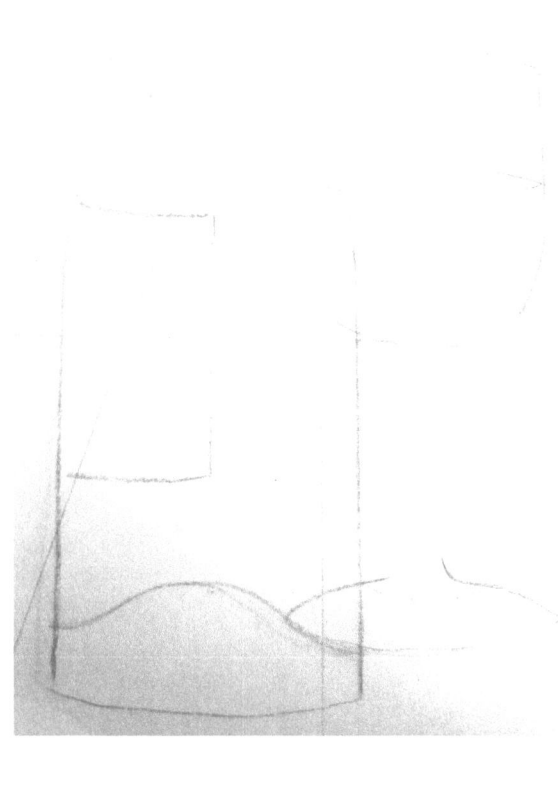

Firstly, using a pastel pencil, draw the outlines of a bottle and glass. To help you get the symmetry correct, you can use a template. A folded piece of tracing paper or lightweight photo-copy paper. Cut the shape of the folded paper and you will get an immediately symmetrical shape. (You may call this cheating, but I call it helping !) Over lap the bottle and glass and draw around the template. Draw a table line straight through the objects.
Now we are beginning to Fracture the shapes.

We next add light beams.
For this painting I am going to envisage the light source coming from above.
Draw the lines, equidistant from each other to get a pleasing symmetry.
Again, the lines go straight through the shapes, breaking up the surface into Fractured.
In this next step, we add on lines in a less obvious way.
I look for lines coming off the object which adds extra interest to the painting.

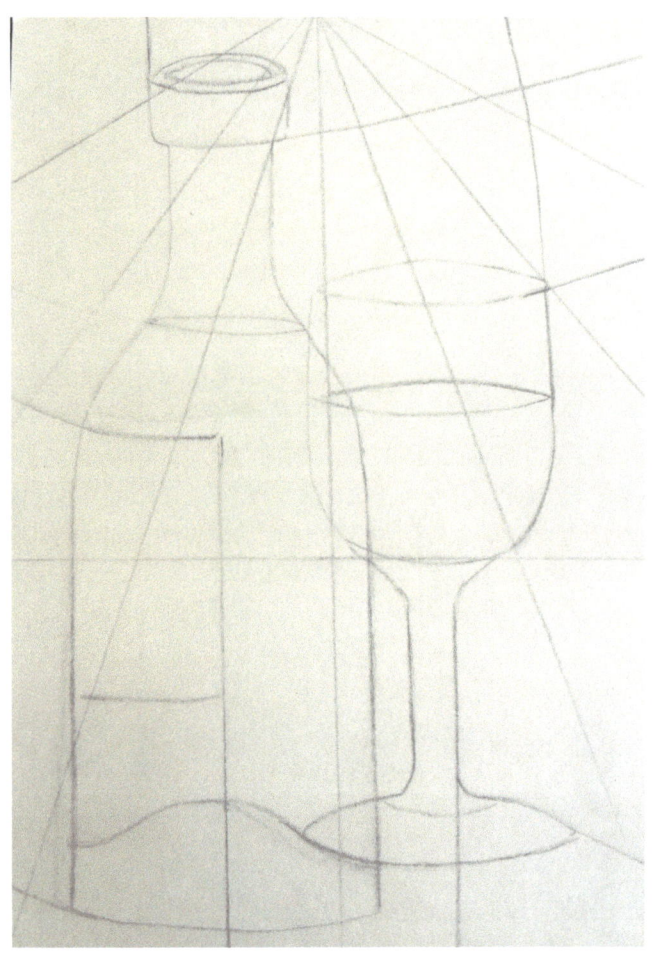

Look at the line coming off from the base of the glass. This breaks up the obvious light beams and creates more interest in the image. If there is a section which is too large, try and see if there's a line which can be extended off and into the space.

Choose your pink, white, pale pink and lilac pastels to begin to fill the background.

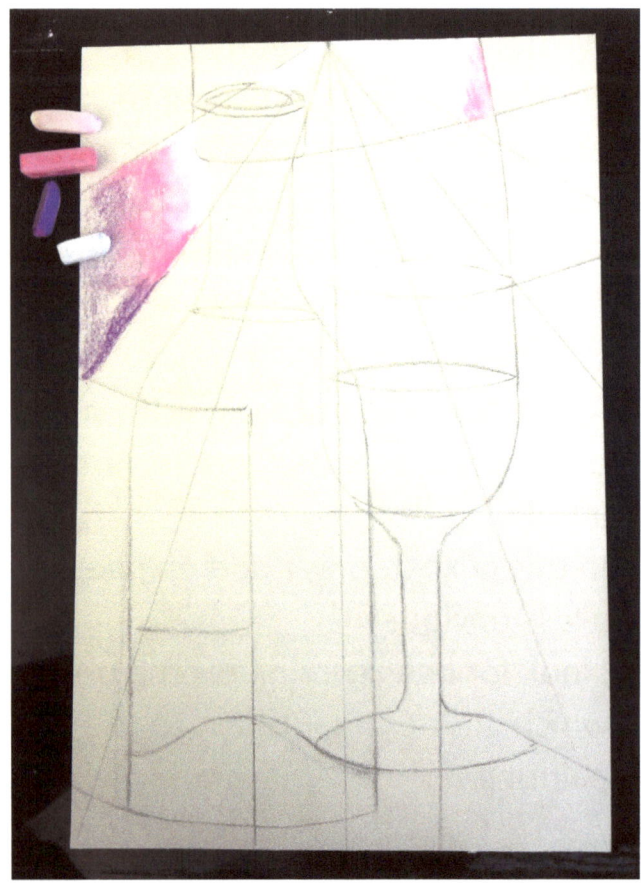

I like to do the background first as then I can establish my tones and depth. You don't have to do this, but I find it helpful to do so.

Start at the very top with white, with gentle strokes, and as you go down the picture, on each Fracture, use the white, pale pink, pink and then lilac.

Blend from light to dark, top to bottom, as you can see in this photo above.

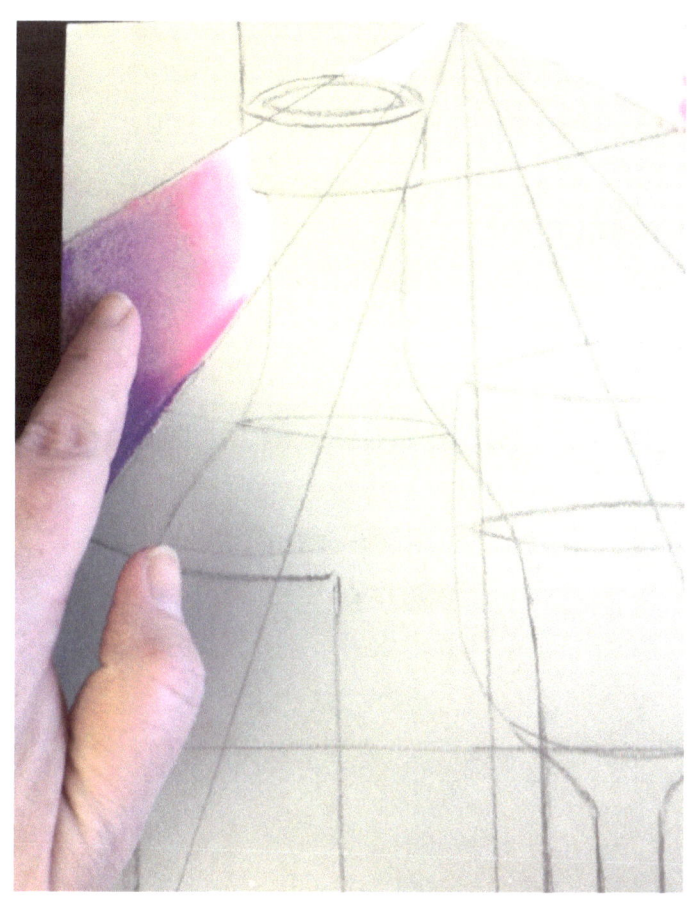

When you have added enough pastel colour to that section and paper, blend it together.
I prefer to use my finger as I like the control I get. However, if you don't like getting dirty fingers, you could use a paper stump or a sponge blender. (it looks like an eye shadow applicator!)
These are also handy for getting into the corners neatly.

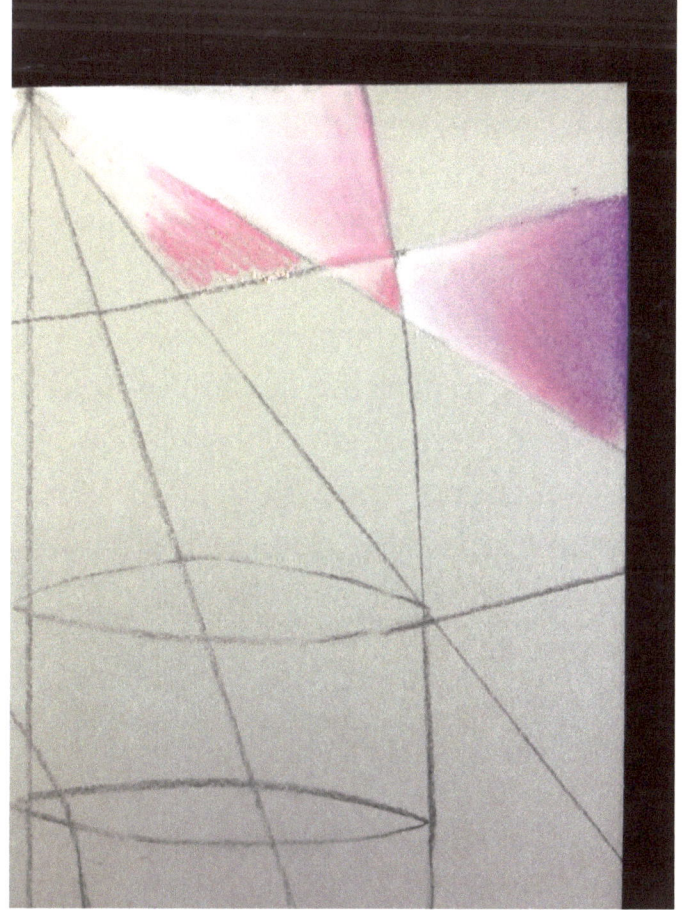

The most important part of Fracturing, and achieving this effect is to make sure each edge has a different tone and colour to it.
You want to make each section work in its own right and keep each area defined.
This close up above shows this. Where the edges meet, there is a clearly shown different colour and tone.
To sharpen the edges, run your finger down the join to smooth it together.
Keep it sharp!

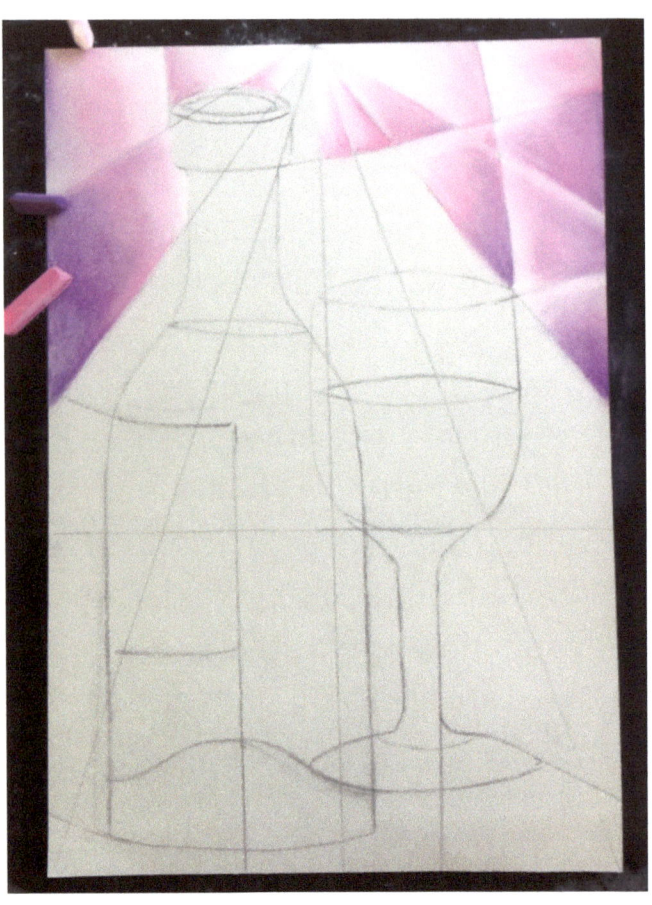

Gradually build up and fill in each section with your pastels. Blending each section smoothly, making sure the colours are smooth and graduated.
Keep the light to dark rule going all the way down the paper.
Please note– This is the way I use pastels. Some artists prefer not to blend, which is of course fine!
It's all to do with personal taste.
If you don't want to blend, then don't! I just think it works best this way.

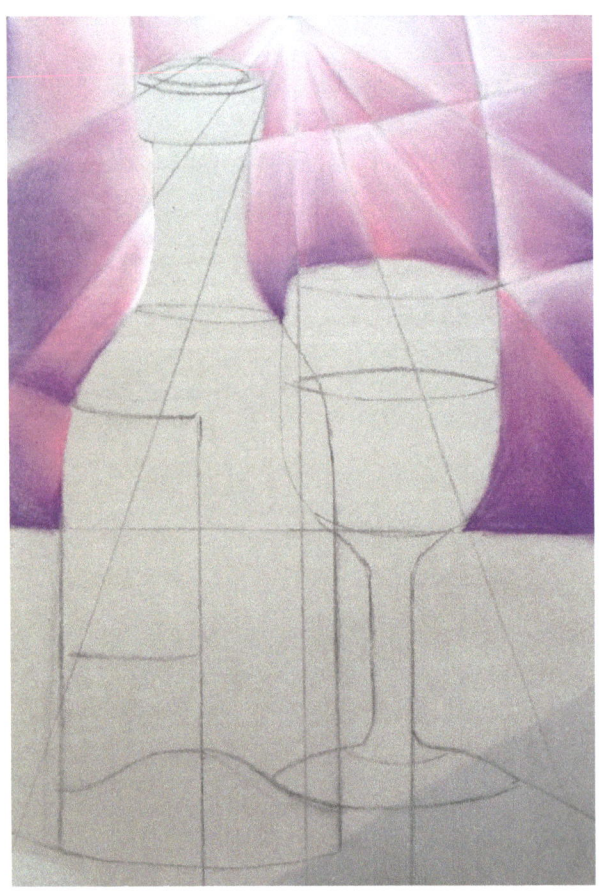

Even though we are making a semi abstract paintings, I still want to keep some rules.
I want the light to dissipate behind the table, giving the object something to sit on.
I also want to give the illusion of a bottle and glass being cylindrical, which of course, they are!
The top of the table need to be light, as if the light is hitting the tabletop.

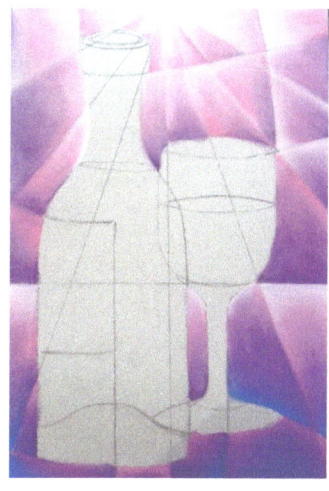
Complete the background. We now use the Indigo, Cerulean and grey pastels

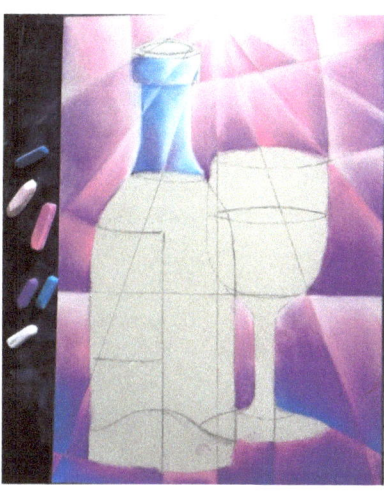
Cover the bottle with pastel, and imagine where the light hits the object. It will be lighter at the top.

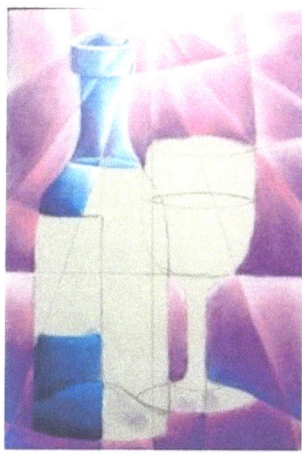
Go darker down at the bottom of the bottle, where there is no light source.

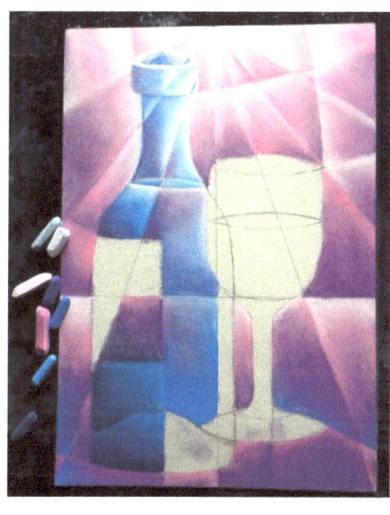
Finish the bottle. Add more indigo at the base, but also include some purple.

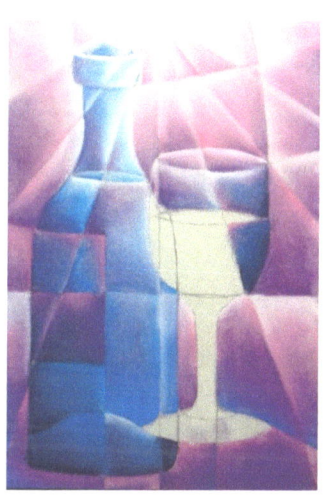
Start the glass. Keep the rim the lightest colour, going darker as you go down.

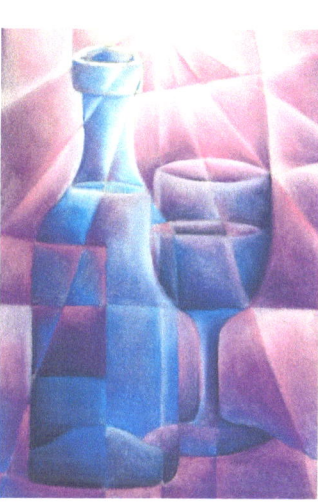
When filled in, tighten the edges and add depth to areas which need defining.

Points to make Fracturing work

The key to making this picture 'pop' is the definition of each section.
Make the edges sharp and crisp.
Blend the colours in a smooth and uniformed way, with no obvious heavy flat colour on each section. Blend, blend, blend.
Keep imagining where your light source is coming from. Light at the top, dark at the bottom.
Make sure the same colour or depth don't meet at each edge.
Draw the lines *off* the object you are drawing. If you don't, then the flow of the Fracture won't work. This is very important!
Keep the perspective correct, we're only making it semi-abstract

Here are 4 paintings completed in a similar way, but using different colours. The effects are all different!

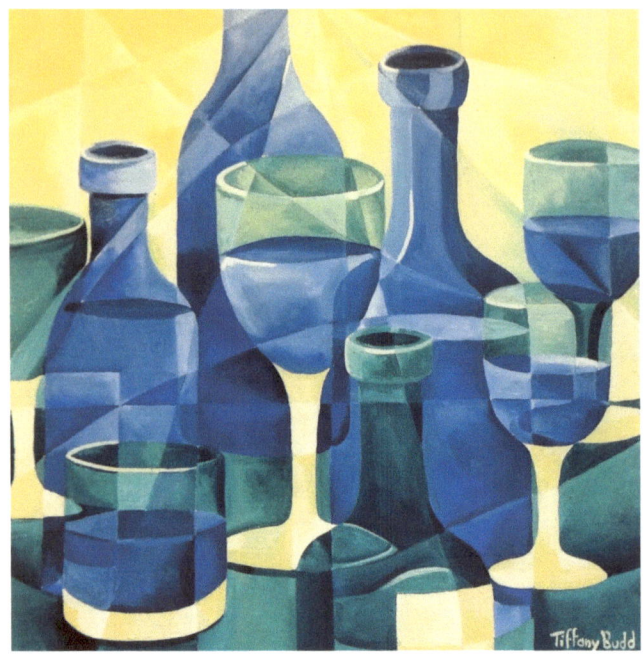
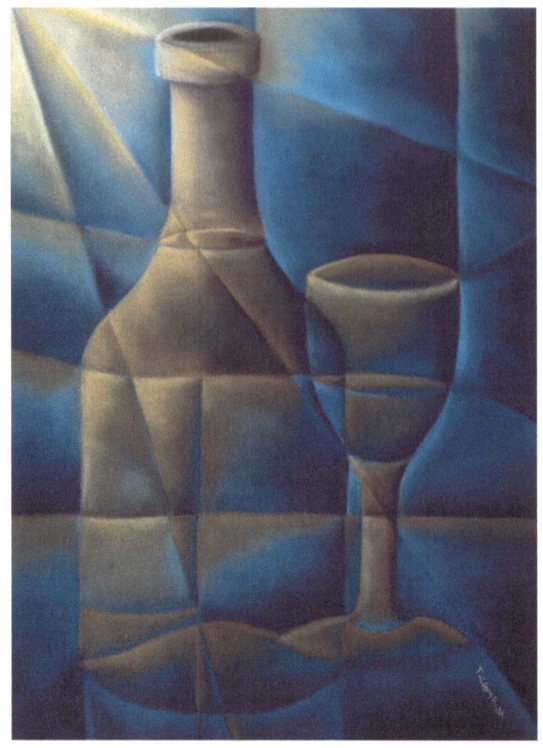
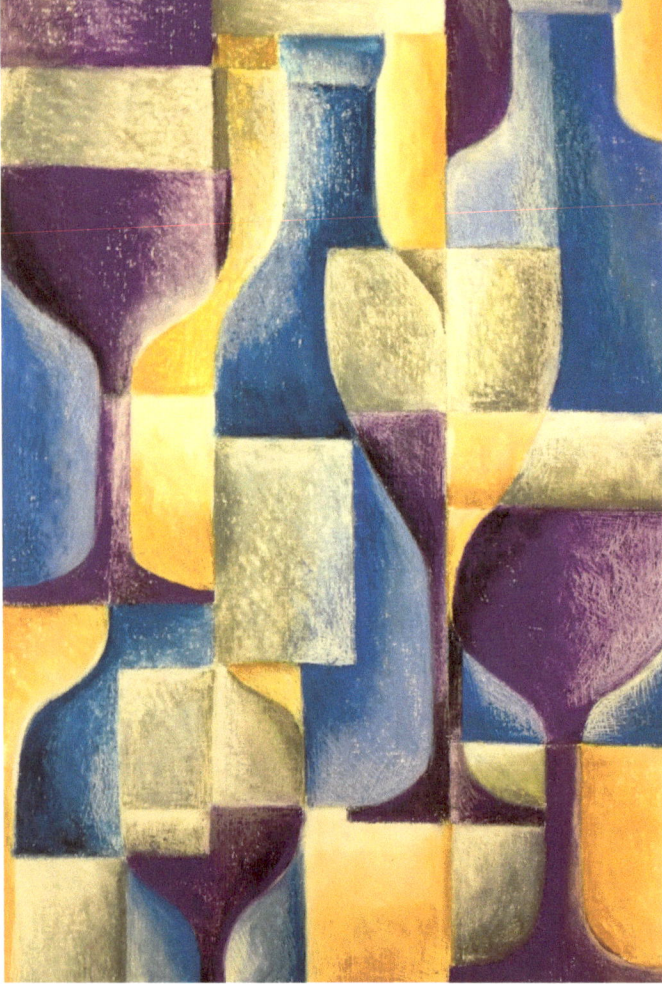
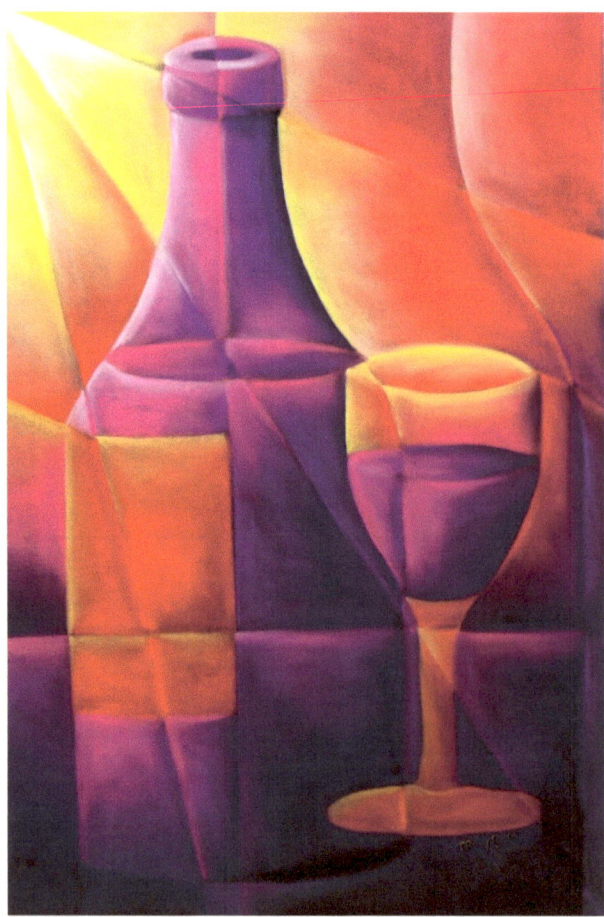

Try different colours, tonal, contrasting and complementary. Experiment with your palette and have some fun!

Fractured Landscapes

Next I am going to show you how to create a Fractured landscape. This is great fun!
When I start these paintings, I imagine that each field or road is full of harvest or flowers The farmers fields are almost Fractured anyway, so it's not too challenging. But keep the flow smooth and the colours exciting. It could be based on an actual place, or be totally imaginary!
Here are some examples of previous paintings I have completed.
They are a mix of watercolour, pastel, acrylic, coloured pencil and graphite.

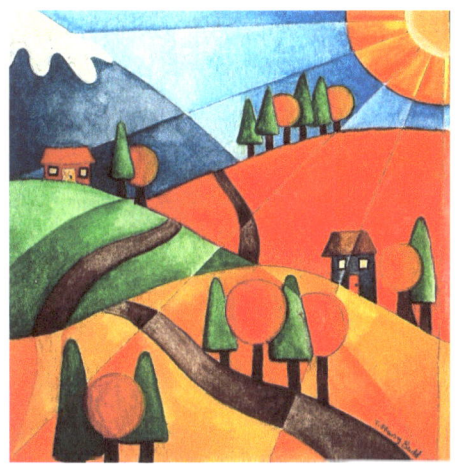

Fractured Sunshine Hills– Watercolour

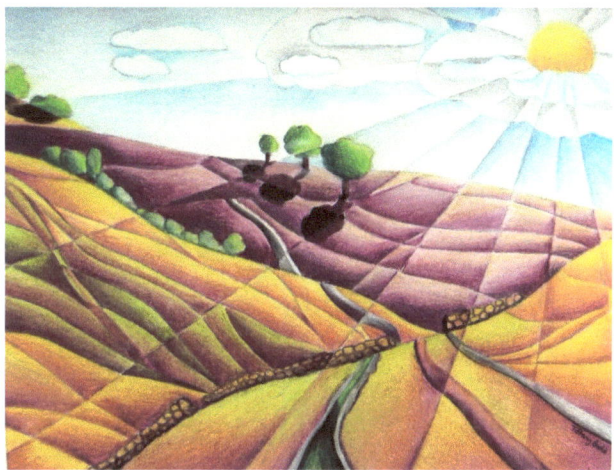

Cressbrook Dale– Coloured Pencil

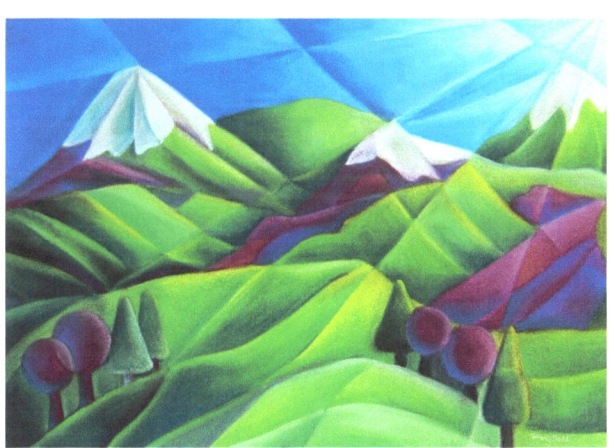

Purple Mountains– Pastel

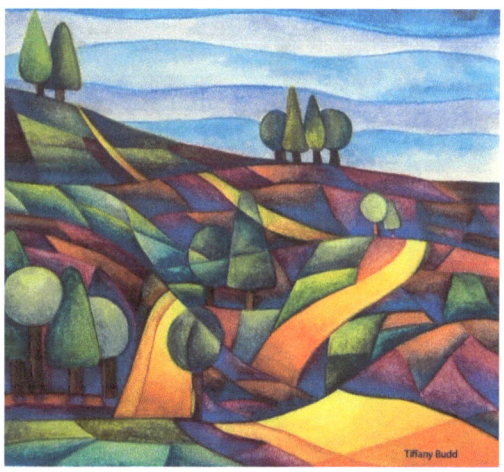

Patchwork Hillside– Watercolour pencils..

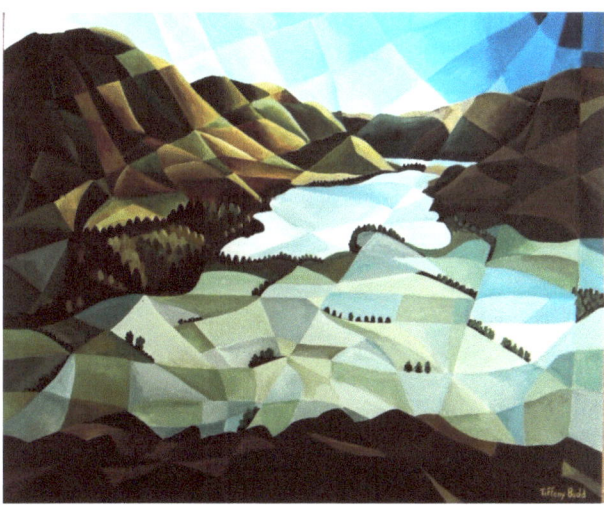

Crummock Water– Acrylic

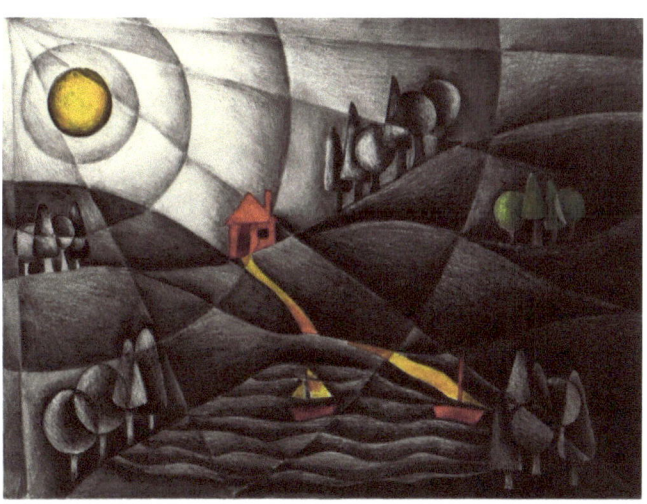

The Path– Graphite and coloured pencils

How to create this painting– using acrylic.
The Colour Hills

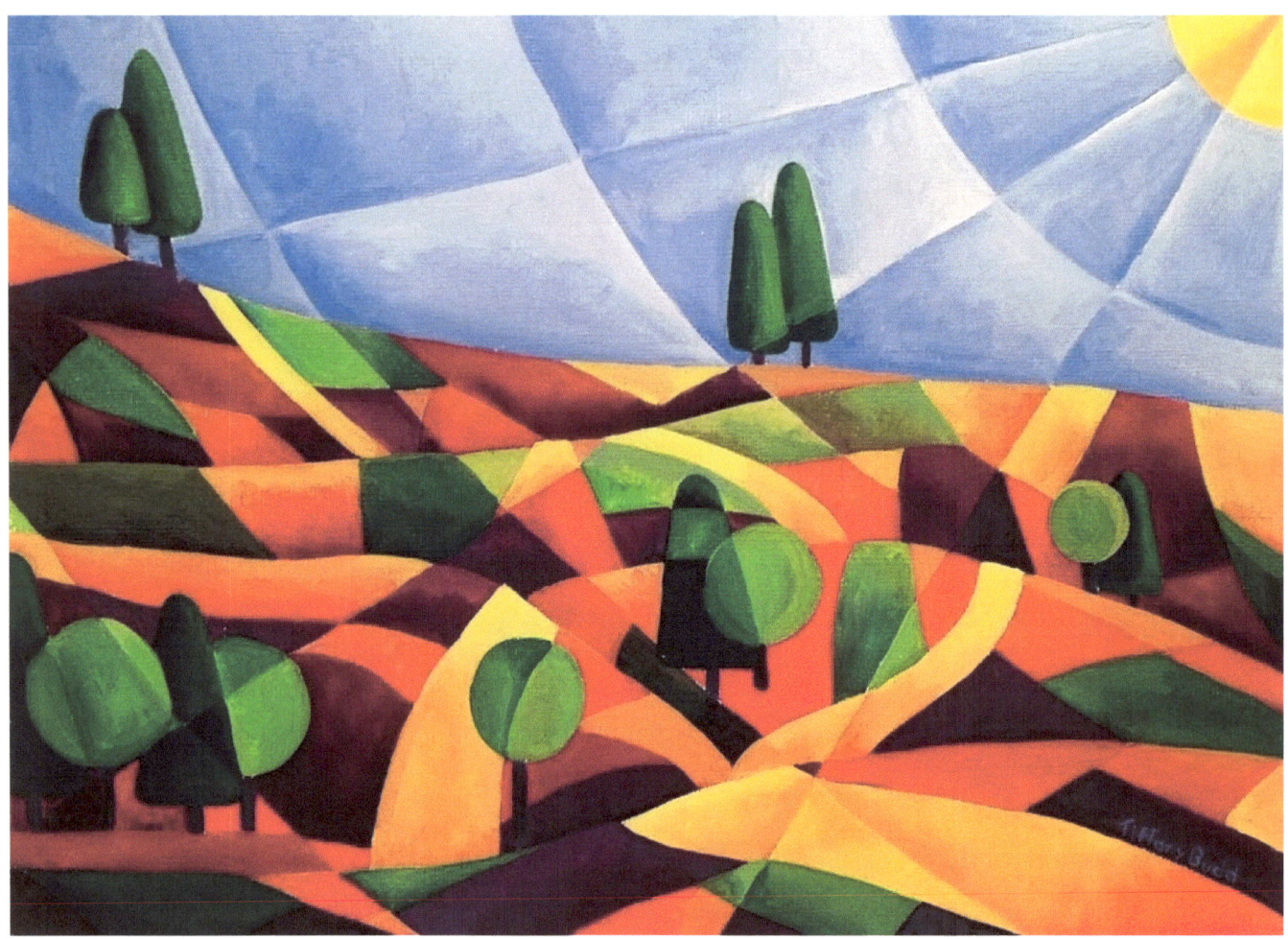

In the next few pages I will show you how I painted this Fractured landscape using acrylic paint. It is bright and cheerful and will make a statement in any room!
If you want to use oil paint, then please do. I personally prefer acrylics and they are odour free and dry quite fast. You can purchase water based oils, which are also good to use.

You will need:-

Suitable canvas or canvas paper- I used System 3 acrylic paper. 30cm Ruler-
Acrylic Brushes- oo to 2
Paint colours
Atelier Interactive Acrylics
Titanium White
Arylamide Yellow Light
Transparent Perinone Orange Crimson
Dioxazine Purple
French Ultramarine
Pthalo Green and Permanent Green Light

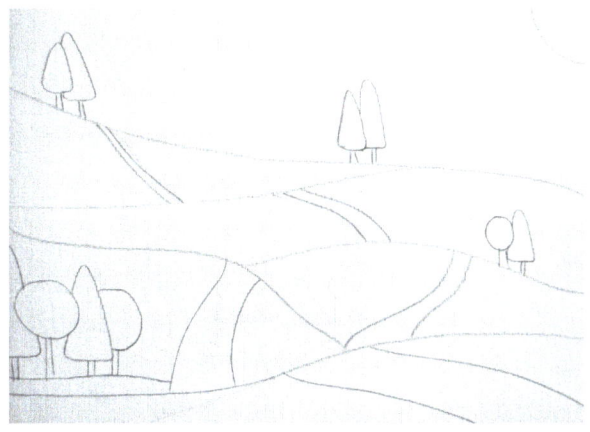

Draw your lines using a graphite pencil, making sure all your lines flow smoothly. I like to add a pathway to show the depth and perspective, from narrow at the back to foreground.

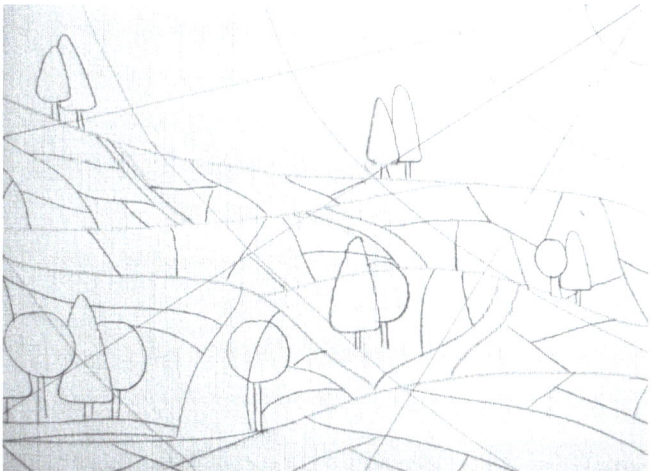

Draw in the light direction using a simple stylised sun. Using your ruler, add the light beams coming out so they look like echo's. Fracturing the picture even more. You have

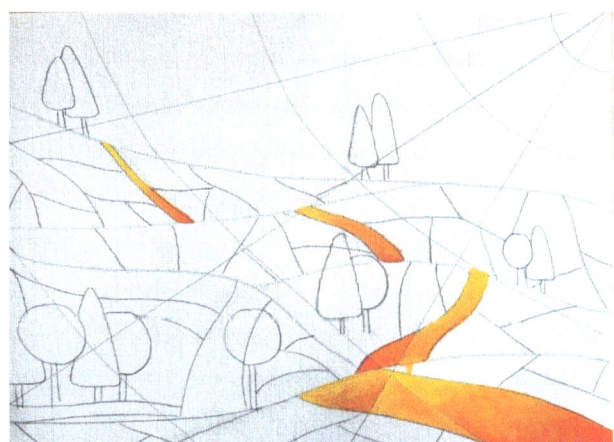

Start with the path. This gives you an idea of the depth and perspective of the pain ting. Deepen the colours as the path heads downwards into the hill dips.

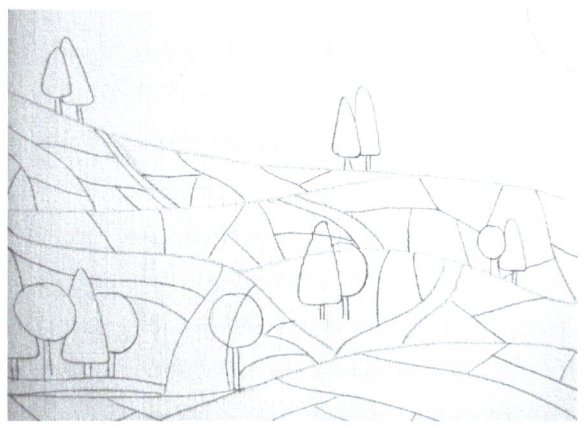

Imagine you're looking at farmers fields in late summer and the landscape is all patch worked. This is nature Fracturing it for us!

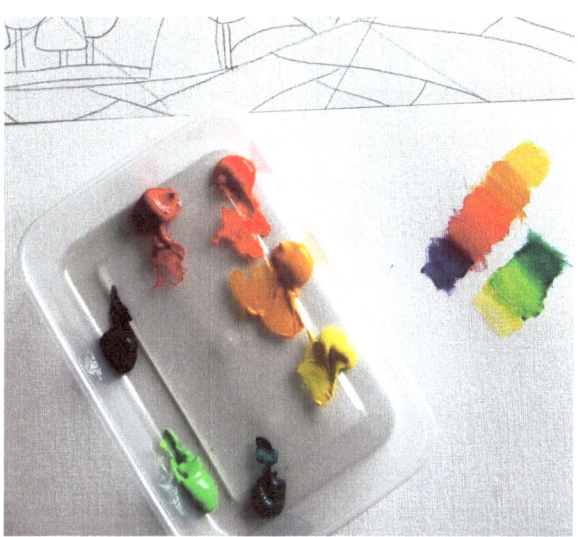

Now, get your paints ready! I use a take away box to store my paint, as it keeps the paint wet for weeks and weeks! So if you don't use it all this time, you can save it for another painting.

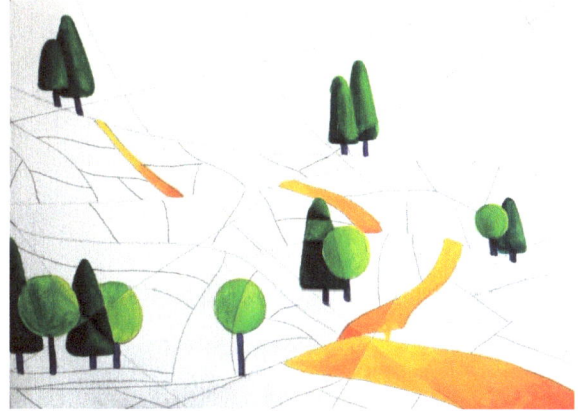

Now to add the trees. These are also stylised. Make sure your colours are dark and light, keep an eye on the lines and remember to keep the tones differently against each line.

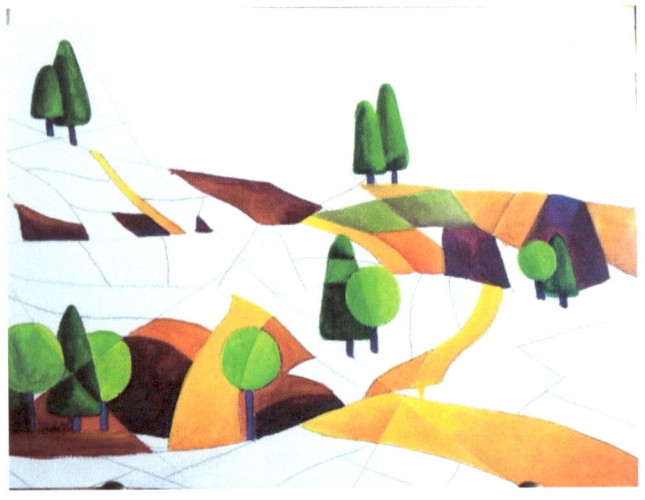
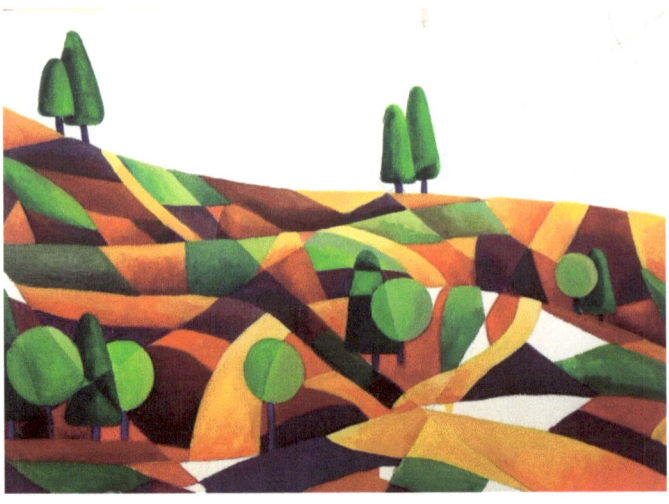

Here come the fields! Think of harvest time, when all the areas are distinctive and colourful. Remember each section needs to be different and tones go from dark to light.

Build up your patchwork hills, darkening the colours as the hills undulate to create shadows and depth.

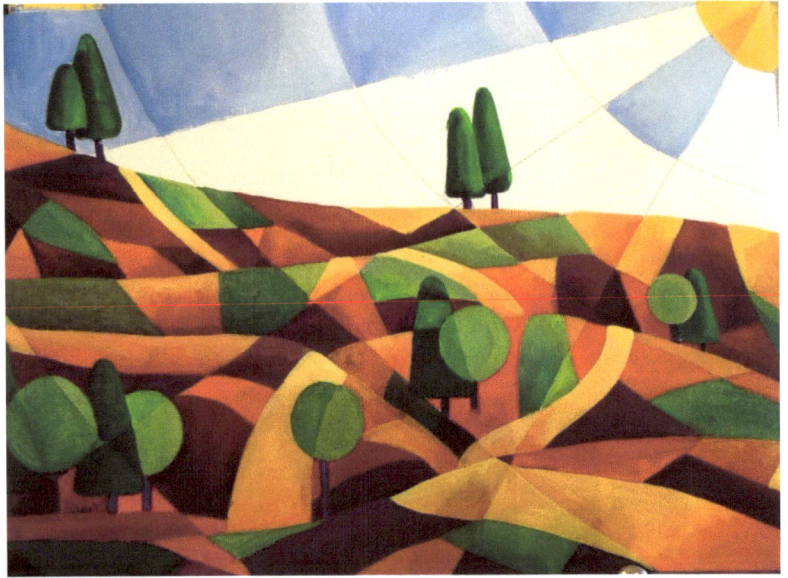

Mix up some Ultramarine blue and Titanium white and begin the blue sky.

Again treating each section with light to dark, going lighter towards the sun.

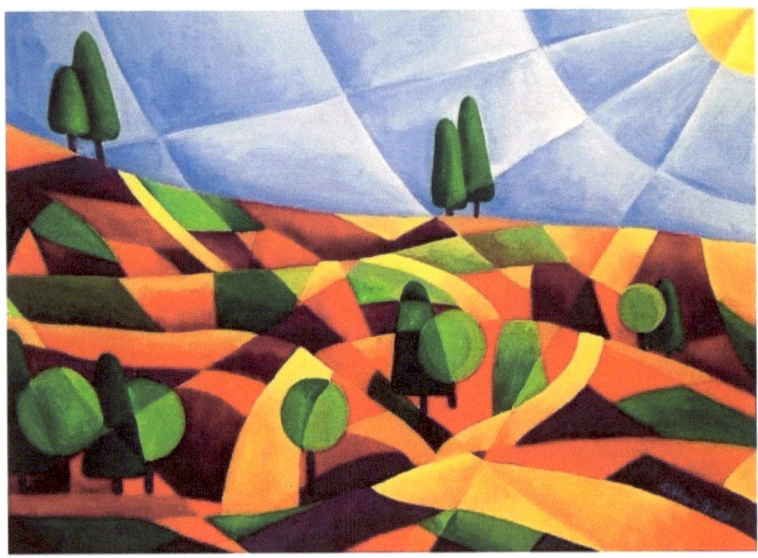

And now take a step back and look at your painting.

Are your colours all blended?

Does each section work well?

Are there any shapes which jump out too much?

Tighten all the edges and make it pop!!

If you've got to grips with this exercise, the have a go at creating your own landscape. Either from a photo of your own, or your imagination! Create those pillows of colour!

Another favourite subject of mine, is fish! I find they sell really well and are great fun to draw.

How I created 'The Pond' using coloured pencils.

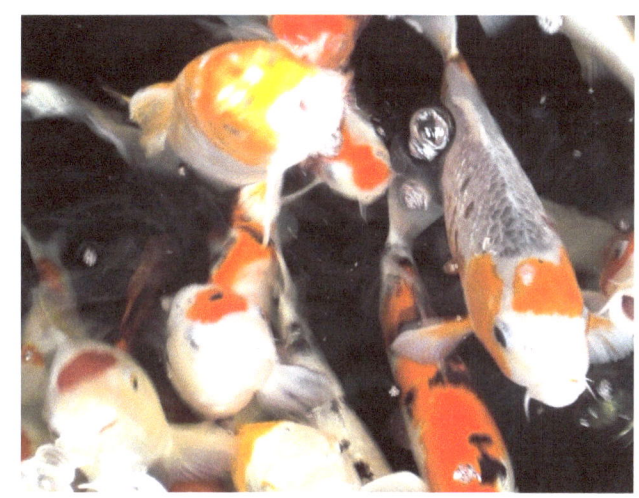

My next work in progress which I am going to show you, is how I created 'The Pond'.
A large and detailed coloured pencil drawing of stylised fish.
I love the way they swim, move and flow through the water.
My inspiration was from a selection of random photos I took whilst at a garden centre in the aquatic department.

I would take lots of photos of the goldfish and carp swimming in the water, catching the reflections and shapes. I took these reference photos and sketched an idea in my trusty sketchbook. My aim in this piece is to evoke the movement and flow of the fish.
I really enjoy the way these fish move and dart about. Once I drew the fish, in different directions and shapes onto the paper, I would then absorb myself completely into it and think about the way they moved and made my 2H pencil follow my thoughts. I find this part so exciting. I never really know how it's going to end up. I also wanted to make shapes which would reflect the sun glistening on the top of the water. I think this part was of upmost importance to add another layer of movement and light.

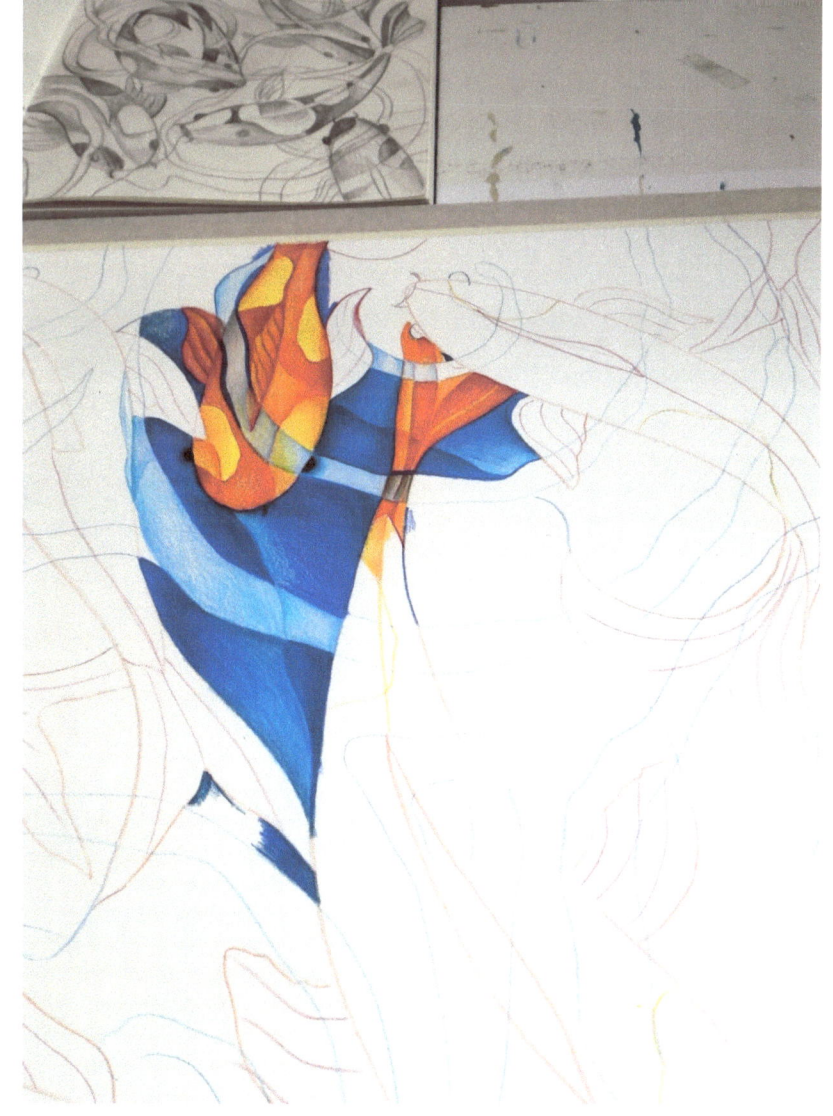

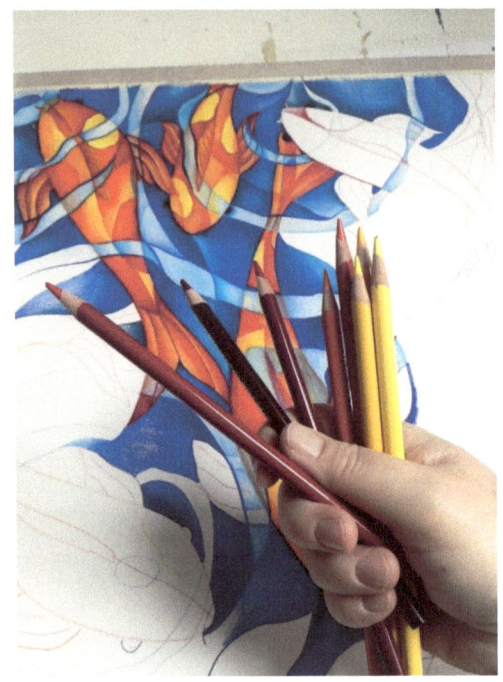

I selected my colours to begin with. A combination of reds, oranges, yellows, blues and greys. I layer my colours, drawing in multiple directions creating a cross hatching effect, until no lines are noticeable. I work with all the colours and complete one section at a time, rather than doing bits all over the paper. I can then see how the balance of colour and shapes work.

As the end is in sight, the paper is beginning to be filled with glorious colour and movement! The blending needs to be smooth. I don't want any scratchy lines or pencil texture to distract from the shapes and shading. I blend with using white or with Derwent's Blender pencil, depending on whether I need the lightness of touch and colour or just smoothness of colour.

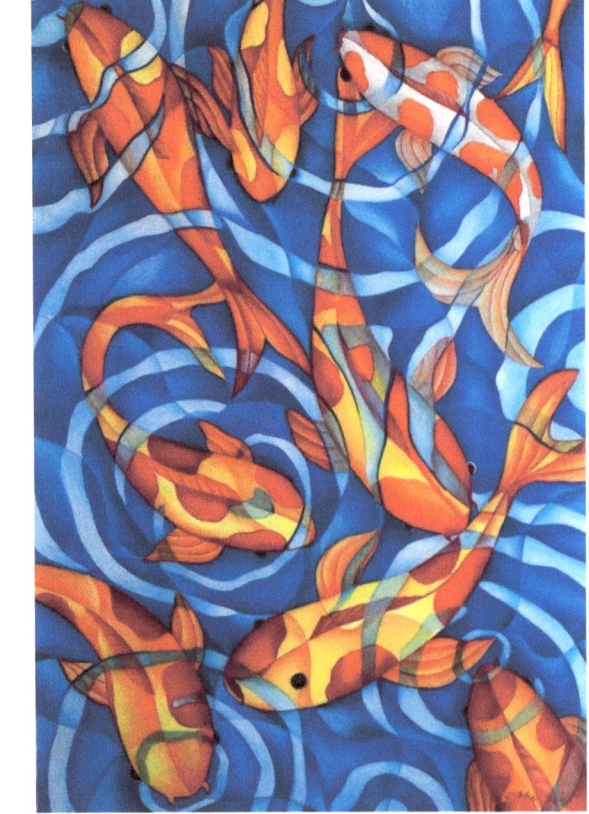

The Pond– by Tiffany Budd

Faber Castell
Coloured pencils.
65cm x 45cm

Variations on my fish theme.

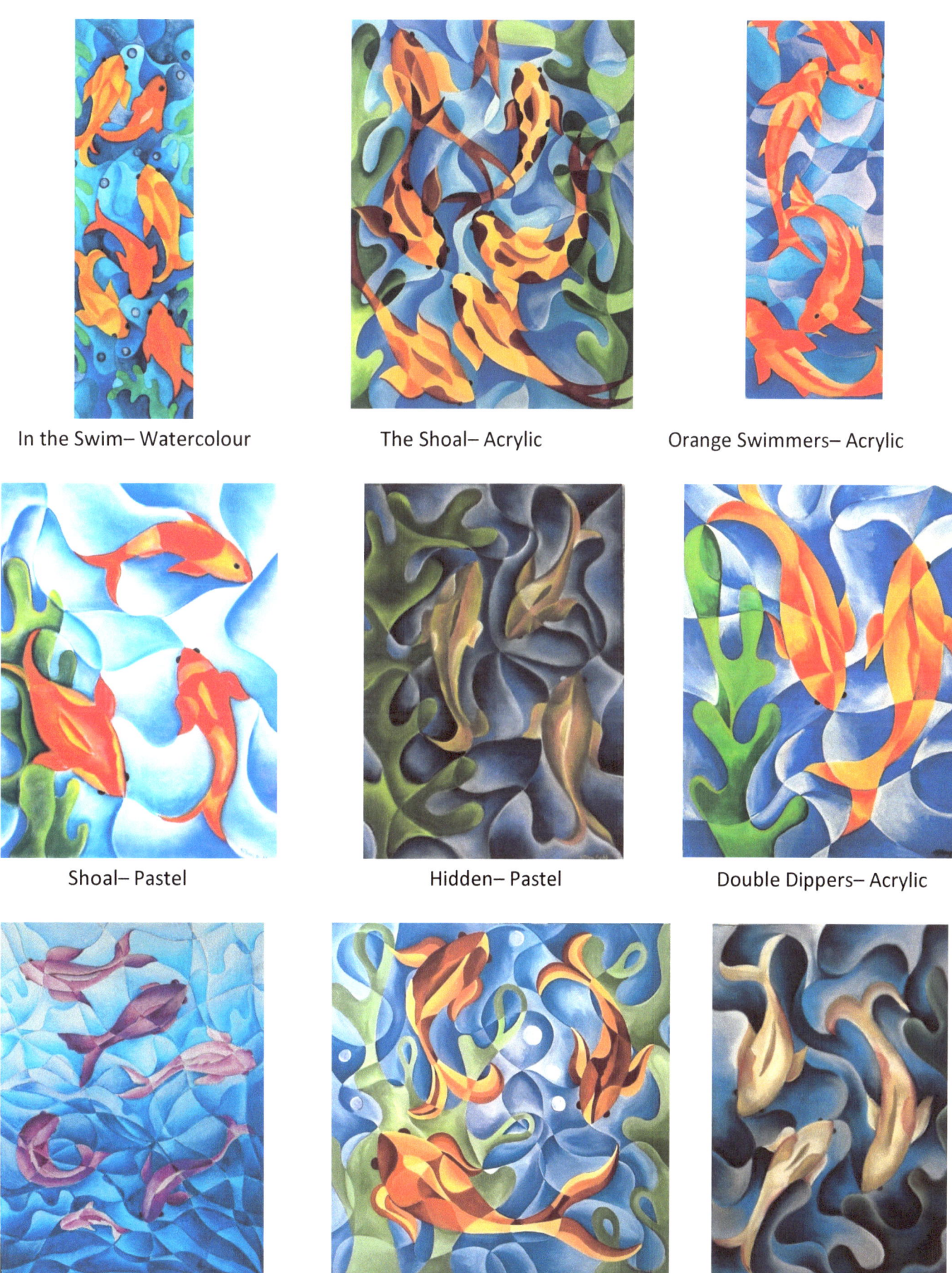

The creation of 'Autumn Abundance' in watercolour pencils.

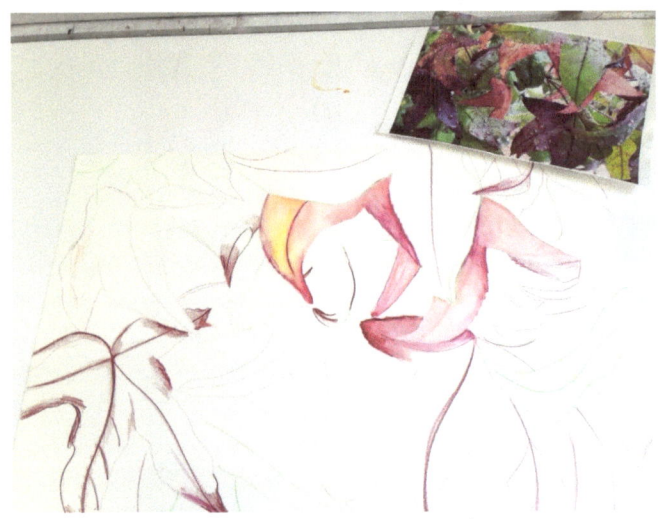

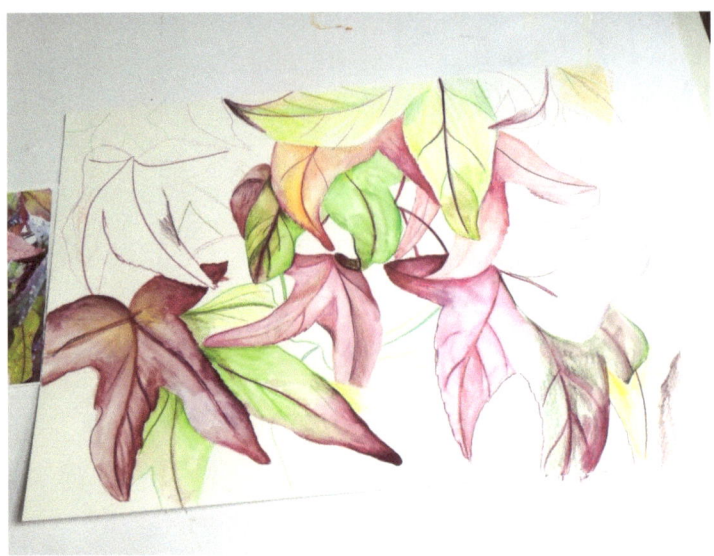

I used my reference photo which I took in autumn when I was out walking. The colours were amazing. I wanted to recreate it using watercolour pencils and in my Fractured style. I did an initial pencil outline of the actual leaf shapes and began to layer the colours. Using watercolour pencils means you can add a water first to lay down some colour which gives it a translucent feel.

I gradually added more washes to get a pleasing colour balance. I then drew with the pencils over the top of the wash with about four colours.

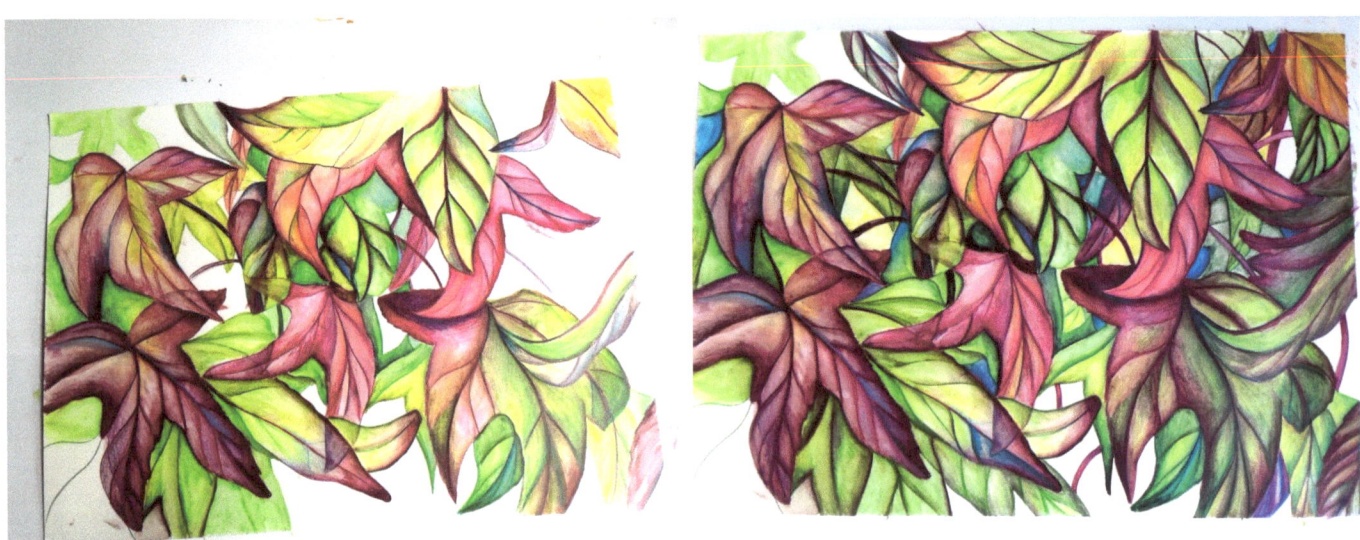

I used a very heavy paper for this drawing. It was a Fabriano Artistico smooth paper which is almost like card and has a very smooth finish. When using watercolour pencils it is advisable to use a heavy base. It takes many layers of pencil and water as sometimes the paper can buckle and begin to disintegrate. Always choose a good quality support. You work hard creating these drawings and paintings, so choose a strong base.

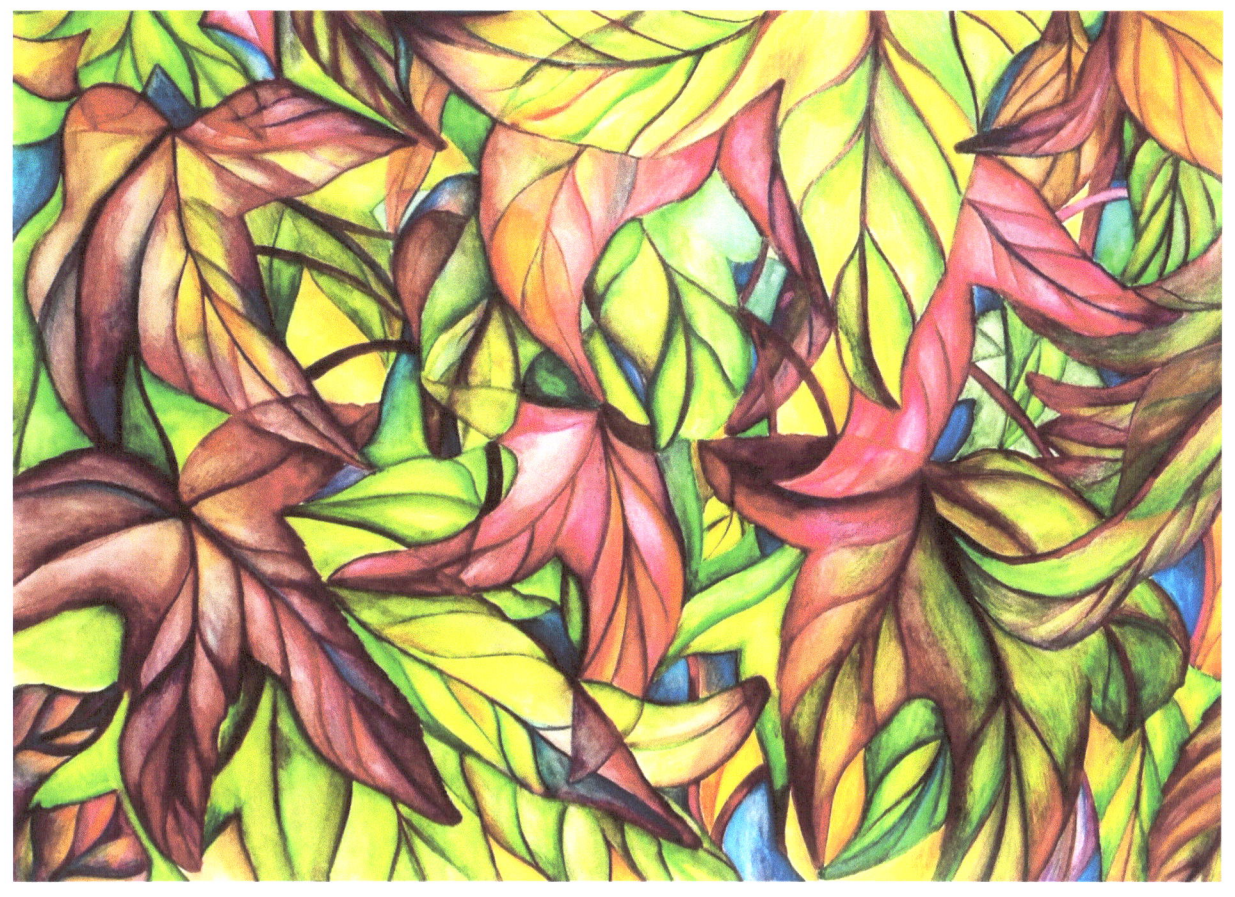

And here is the completed drawing. Full of depth and movement.
Autumn Abundance–
70cm x 50cm. Caran D'Ache Museum Aquarelle pencils.

I do hope you have enjoyed this second version of my very first book.
Please follow me on Facebook and Twitter for regular updates.
And also take a look at my grown up colouring books all available on Amazon.

www.tiffanybudd.co.uk   All images Copyright ©Tiffany Budd 2017

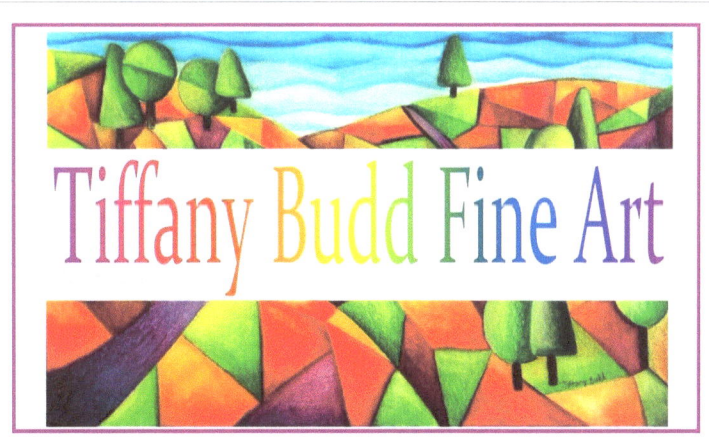

www.ingramcontent.com/pod-product-compliance
Lightning Source LLC
Chambersburg PA
CBHW051837210526
45473CB00005B/1921